PAMPHLETS ON AMERICAN WRITERS • NUMBER 22

UNIVERSITY OF MINNESOTA

✓ *Recent American Novelists*

BY JACK LUDWIG

UNIVERSITY OF MINNESOTA PRESS • MINNEAPOLIS

Printed in the United States of America at
the Jones Press, Inc., Minneapolis

Library of Congress Catalog Card Number: 62-63700

Second printing 1966

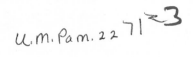

Distributed to high schools in the United States by
McGraw-Hill Book Company, Inc.

New York   Chicago   Corte Madera, Calif.   **Dallas**

PUBLISHED IN GREAT BRITAIN, INDIA, AND PAKISTAN BY THE OXFORD
UNIVERSITY PRESS, LONDON, BOMBAY, AND KARACHI, AND IN
CANADA BY THOMAS ALLEN, LTD., TORONTO

FOR HARRY AND LEAH KATZ

JACK LUDWIG, short story writer, novelist, and critic, is a professor of English at the new Long Island Center of the State University of New York.

Recent American Novelists

THE novel, like civilization, is from time to time pronounced dead, and yet, like civilization, somehow keeps going.
The novel died first with Fielding, then with Dickens, Flaubert,
Dostoevski, Tolstoi, died again with Proust, and with Joyce, and,
most recently, with Hemingway. A pride of friendly critics has
always stood ready to be the novel's pallbearers: F. R. Leavis, in
The Great Tradition, praised the novel so highly and defined it
so rigorously that its death seemed unavoidable. Other critics
brought slightly jollier news of the novel as moribund, ailing, or
irrelevant. Lionel Trilling, for instance, suggests that the post-
World War II novel is an anomaly, perhaps an archaism, since
its function, he says, has been taken over by David Riesman sociology which does what the novel should do, but doesn't, better.

Sickness, even unto death, in the U.S.A. is no guarantee of freedom from exhortation: what's left in America of the *avant-garde*
rallies contemporary novelists to the twenties' measure of modernity, technical innovation, suggesting the smart writer would do
well to imitate industry's planned obsolescence and retool stylistically every few years, and thus assure himself, in these 1960's, a
fictional equivalent of electronic music, action painting, computers, and megaton bombs. Mass-media celebrators of this as
"The American Century," like, say, the editors of *Life*, blast contemporary writers for wasting the unlimited advertising opportunities of a 500-page novel, each leaf a potential showcase, or
billboard, for numberless "The American Way of Life" commer-

cials. The novelist is variously worshiped and admonished for trying to be, and not trying to be, philosopher, theologian, social chronicler, group therapist, Messiah. Though the novel is often declared dead a potentially vast audience awaits — perhaps with skepticism — this age's novelistic *Summa Theologica,* a book of the scope of a *War and Peace* or a *Brothers Karamazov,* to sum up twentieth-century America as *The Adventures of Huckleberry Finn* and *Moby Dick* seemed to sum up America the innocent.

America's literary fashion magazines, however, have more modest goals, and in the period since World War II have consistently featured market-tested models of urbanity, sophistication, and compactness: the *New Yorker's* reiterated hero, for instance, a sensitive and slightly depressed searcher for secular communion in unlikely and unholy suburban places, or *Esquire's* eastern-educated world traveler committed to a passionate catalogue of his clothes and his suffering, the latter a combination of fear and guilt about the atomic bomb, sexual ambiguity, and the *gaffe* of being caught in a three-button jacket in a two-button year. Don Quixote, in this world, is a low-energy quester who dreams of knights and wakes to find even his windmills gone, converted, alas, to quaint "Tea Shoppes" along modern America's automotive jousting trails; Sancho, for his part, packs a neat shaving-kit of tranquilizers, and counsels adjustment, acceptance, and what Auden calls "short views."

Fiction's stereotypes account for the rather friendly reception accorded so-called Beat novelists of the last fifteen years. An America conditioned by T. S. Eliot to fear — and feel guilty about — aridity, sterility, impotence, paralysis may be forgiven for confusing Beat howl with lyricism, its violence with vitality, its self-advertisement with self-evaluation. In the Beat New American Dream, Huck Finn has become a hood, Ahab a dope peddler, Natty Bumppo a switch-blade artist slashing his way through the urban wilderness. The message is as direct and simple as a singing commercial: the Beat hero would be a better person if only the world would come through, first, and be a better place. Since the world, as the Beat analysis of the contemporary crisis invariably proves, is bad, this hero has a solemn obligation, evidently, to make it worse. Crime is, unsurprisingly, a duty; the criminal is this corrupt world's only possible saint; he alone affirms the Life Force and what the Beat writer frequently refers to as love. Liberated from the factual tyranny of history, the Beat writer can salute as brilliant inventions the staler eclecticisms of nineteenth-century nihilists — ignorance, like incoherence and illiteracy, is flashy proof of flight beyond the suppression of categorical imperatives. The Beat novel spangles a chintzy weave of souvenir strands — handbook Kierkegaard, outline Nietzsche, synoptic Camus, fragment Freud, *lumpen*-Zen Buddhism, tenth-remove Existentialism, fiftieth-remove Christ. The Decline of the West is, instead of lamented, exemplified.

But the Beat novel is an Alexandrian symptom of something serious and important in American society and American fiction; the tolerance accorded Beat oversimplification and simple-mindedness reflects an uneasiness in the postwar world, an impatience and dissatisfaction with the fashionable novel's self-limiting and self-justifying scope. Serious fiction shows definite signs of turning from the Kafkaesque "Underground Man" to a Tolstoian or Conradian "Aboveground Man," the hero who breaks out of his real, or symbolic, sealed-off room to re-enter the world of action and history. A generation which has known Hitler, and Stalin, Hiroshima, and Korea, is forced beyond the vision of Kafka, the pose of the Underground Man, the lament of Ecclesiastes.

The great change in the focus and tone of American fiction is dramatized in the work of this generation's leading novelist Saul Bellow, whose first two books, *Dangling Man* (1944) and *The*

7

Victim (1947), belong to the tradition of the Underground Man. Where American fiction of the 1930's by a Dos Passos, a Steinbeck, a Farrell would claim man is a victim of *the* villain, "The System" — industrial society, capitalism, the managers — Bellow early in his career suggests the villain is God (or whatever it is that has made man's existence largely a matter of suffering). The agony is real, the villain vague, though vast. Poverty is not, as in the 1930's, the curse from which man can liberate himself through political action, organization, or revolution; poverty, instead, is part of the vast conspiracy of humiliation which Bellow's spiritual sad-sack "hero," Joseph, in *Dangling Man*, ingloriously but endlessly catalogues. Friends are introduced to betray, wives to fall short, work to frustrate; the sky and the sun and the stars exist to mock man's littleness, his dullness, his earth-bound insignificance. Job, the message seems to be, at least had boils to show for his pains; Joseph, only indignities.

Joseph, as a characteristic Bellow hero, doesn't achieve stature through talent, power, position, sensitivity, wisdom, or any other traditional heroic equipment: he, an unaccomplished Faustus, reaches high only through brassy expectation. His ambition, he says, is to "sound creation," not because that is what man should do but because of his needs. "O.K., God," he seems to be saying, "if your creation is as hot as you say it is how come it can't bring *me* to life?"

At this stage in Bellow's fictional career he does not yet make use of the rich ironic possibilities of a Joseph's attitudes. He sees nothing unusual, it seems, in Joseph's conception of the war as a therapy of violence which "could teach me . . . what I had been unable to learn . . . in the room." Joseph preserves a delightful one-to-one relationship with the entire universe: the proof that anything exists is its ability to strike fire from *his* stoniness. The universe, not Bellow's hero, is in need of an existential demonstration. As Joseph unsmilingly declares at the end of the book, "The next move was the world's." A new heroic concept: the world needs the hero more than the hero needs the world.

The form of *Dangling Man* is a journal, the place of action a room — or, more precisely, Joseph's mind. He is not one of the "hardboiled," who live by "the code of the athlete" and "fly planes or fight bulls or catch tarpon." Joseph, for exercise, only contends with God.

Bellow, possibly America's most intellectual novelist ever, sets his action and his heroic at a polar extreme from Hemingway's. Let Hemingway, like God, create legends: Bellow, at this stage of his career, prefers less to create than discuss. Not the "author" of Genesis but the Talmudic sages who dissect it are his forebears.

In Bellow's second novel, *The Victim,* Talmudic wit is still present, still lacking the characteristic irony of an uncynical acceptance of man's potential absurdity — particularly in attempting argument with God. The idea of the victim is the key to the hero in all of Bellow's novels — Joseph in *Dangling Man,* Asa Leventhal in *The Victim,* Augie in *The Adventures of Augie March*, Wilhelm in *Seize the Day*, Henderson in *Henderson the Rain King,* Herzog in Bellow's forthcoming novel: the "victim" is he who can blame his suffering or failure on somebody or something outside of himself. This is, for the most part, the stance set up by Bellow's hero against the world. Asa Leventhal has a wider range of lament and accusation than Joseph of *Dangling Man,* but his target is still whoever it is "who runs things." Human communion, the book's conclusion seems to say, comes from mortal enemies embracing in a oneness reached only when they focus on the villain "who runs things," and whose evil makes theirs, in comparison, small potatoes. Asa, like Joseph, has scored against the creation, his proof of its inadequacy similar to Joseph's —

9

that nothing-of-a-creation did *not* liberate Asa from the prison of spiritual deadness. Asa, like Joseph, first covers his eyes before rainbows and then laments the world's colorlessness; God created the heavens and the earth for man yesterday, but what has he done for man *today?*

The world of *The Victim* is larger than a room or Asa's mind. Contiguous with Joseph, an extension of him, perhaps, Asa is Joseph moved from a room to a city. That enervating one-to-one relationship between Joseph and not-Joseph (for how else is one to differentiate Bellow's hero from his environment?) has been enlarged, if not greatly extended. Joseph's world was as unfurnished as a Kafka hero's — colorless, shapeless, airless, ahistorical. Asa Leventhal lives in a recognizable modern city, New York, and though it doesn't sound New York as Bellow's novella, *Seize the Day*, does, it points to the explosion in Bellow's fiction that soon followed.

That explosion, *The Adventures of Augie March* (1953), signals Bellow's turning, and, equally significant, the novel's. The hero is "aboveground," still, perhaps, only paroled from his underground purview, but unquestionably in the real world. Augie is, like Joseph and Asa, a victim, but he, unlike them, is surrounded by the sounds of creation felt now in the accents and rhythms of Bellow's prose, which turns away from Kafka toward Gogol and Tolstoi and Babel. If Augie fails to "sound creation" Bellow himself does not. The world is no longer a mere proof of his hero's ability to feel, to see, to hear. The world flames out in Bellow's prose, in his rediscovery of the real world — its colors, its sounds, its joy and possible glory. History and the richness of tradition are this novel's new hangings. A multitude of characters appear and make their claims on Augie. Action, more than reflection, becomes the measure of fiction. Bellow, unaffected by the *avant-garde's* urgings-on, has rediscovered Fielding and Balzac and Dickens and Twain and *Moby Dick*'s Melville, has shaken loose of the *avant-garde*'s Kafka pitch, its failure to see beyond technique in *Finnegans Wake*.

The novelist of this generation, with veneration for both Kafka and Joyce, could — if he were fortunate — see that both Kafka and Joyce, on one level, offered the contemporary novelist only fictional dead ends. The despair caught in the Kafka image or parable was his own, and not to be appropriated for literary purposes; similarly Joyce's literary innovations grew out of a peculiar isolation he himself felt as an Irishman writing in what he considered to be a borrowed language, English. His innovation tried to create a language he alone could define and control, a language he thought was independent of English. Regardless, though, Kafka and Joyce, when imitated, end up being aped. Bellow's *Augie March* clearly recognizes the dead end and, as clearly, rejoins the novel's high-road. More than that, it reaffirms the novel's roots in what Conrad called "the visible world." By implication, *Augie March* declares what Bellow's heroes may never achieve — recognition of man's legends as inexhaustible, his variety and complexity infinite. *Augie March* re-enters the world: places are charmed into life, history becomes a dimension of a hero's awareness — if not yet his acts.

Augie from his opening words celebrates the epiphanies of this world, including his own failure and, characteristically, his own fated victim-role. "I am an American, Chicago born — Chicago, that somber city — and go at things as I have taught myself, free-style, and will make the record in my own way: first to knock, first admitted . . . But a man's character is his fate, says Heraclitus, and in the end there isn't any way to disguise the nature of the knocks by acoustical work on the door or gloving the knuckles." Augie March is the first Bellow hero who would recognize a significant life if it stood before him. He is Joseph and Asa rehabilitated: *that first try was a flop*, say the therapist's directions, *re-educate yourself, kid, but do it with ebullience.*

Bellow is engaged in his great task — to reconcile man the individual with man the evolution. Or to put it another way, Augie as Culture is now free to misbehave in the higher name of himself as Nature. As an aspiring Life Force man owes himself a Big Destiny, even if it has to be achieved by becoming "hardboiled" and knocking on all doors with undisguised boorishness.

This more querulous Huck, this other-directed Finn, is pushed around by a series of Widows and Tom Sawyers, each furnished out with doctrine or program guaranteed to make Augie something special — i.e., the particular thing each Life-giver has in mind for Augie. But Augie is better at listening than at learning: it's his master faculty, to be able to subject himself to a series of remakers and yet emerge essentially unchanged. What profits from these encounters is Bellow's art and the texture of his novel.

No longer is a character or a place only a one-to-one function of a Bellow hero's complaint or his problem-solving proclivity. To facilitate the turn toward Life, Bellow has Augie complete the trip to the World begun by Asa Leventhal: Augie swings through space with that "free style" he puffs about on the opening page of the novel. And on that swing he sees places and meets people who celebrate themselves and all human possibility quite independent of what they *do* for Augie March. Bellow in *Augie March* gives Chicago the tragic sparkle Joyce lavished on his Dublin. A city becomes a large text where one may read the signature of all things.

Compare the spare drabness of *Dangling Man* with this description of a small-time cornball, Happy Kellerman (who, characteristic of Bellow, is treated generously under the heading of "nose"): "He was a beer *saufer*, droopy, small, a humorist, wry, drawn, weak, his tone nosy and quinchy, his pants in creases under his paunch; his nose curved up and presented offended and timorous nostrils, and he had round, disingenuous eyes in which he showed he was strongly defended. He was a *tío listo,* a carnival type, a whorehouse visitor. His style was that of a hoofer in the lowest circuit, doing a little cane-swinging and heel-and-toe routine . . ." Or this description of something Mexican, which moves easily from concrete detail to philosophical reflection: "bones dug out of the rented graves are thrown on a pile when the lease is up . . . Beggars in dog voices . . . enact the last feebleness for you with ancient Church Spanish . . . The burden carriers with the long lines, hemp lines they wind over their foreheads . . . lie in the garbage at siesta and give themselves the same exhibited neglect the dead are shown. Which is all to emphasize how openly death is received everywhere, in the beauty of the place . . ."

Augie March provides Bellow with an open form, a way of writing *about* almost anything with almost unlimited scope — i.e., the limits are imposed not by the chosen form of the novel, but rather, as they should be, by the author's own limitations of talent, imagination, and knowledge. Bellow himself is writing "free style," and the result is a novel with form so free few commentators have been able to resist the tacky label of "picaresque." Where Asa Leventhal was concerned with solving the problem of *who* runs things, Augie is trying to learn *how* to run things, how to order his life so it has broad human significance. Bellow's fiction has proceeded to actions and dramatic confrontations of sufficient stature to allow for generalization. Augie is, then, Bellow's first Aboveground Man.

American novelists, Bellow included, have always built "escape clauses" into their fictions, have almost always presented heroes with ready-made apology for limitations of profundity, scope, and stature. A writer like J. D. Salinger has the American Adolescent

Factor as his escape clause — i.e., how can you expect anything more from someone so young, so innocent, so unfallen, so immature, etc.? Writers like Fitzgerald had Social Hierarchy and Environmental Factor escape clauses to explain a hero's limited perceptions and involvements. Hemingway extolls The Man of Action (who is not a college professor, mac), which cuts down on a reader's expectation of what a hero could feel and think and talk about. Other writers have used the Common Man or Ordinary Guy escape clause which Bellow, without shame, invokes in *Augie March* by having Augie, whose language is poetic and lyric and dramatic, say, "I'm no writer."

Most American writers feel at home with a hero explicitly inferior to themselves, whose ideas are more naive than the writer's, whose knowledge is less expansive, whose talent is less established. This American tradition is in sharp contrast to the Russian concept of the hero (who apologizes for Ivan Karamazov's reflections, Mitya's struggles with Christian feeling, Marmaladov's vision of the Day of Judgment?), or the French, or even the English. Perhaps the American writer can have his hero serve doubly — once in furthering the democratic myth of the Ordinary Joe; once again in avoiding the challenge to one's imagination and compassion that comes, as it came to, say, Shakespeare in *Hamlet*, from putting one's highest conception of man into fictional action. In *Augie March* Bellow has created a world where a great hero is a possibility; what the book lacks is a hero and an action to rise to the level of Bellow's writing. Augie, like Bellow's later heroes, still is too much of a "dangling man" and "victim." The new dimension, though, is Augie's affirmation of the world around him as a vale of possibility, rather than tears: he is a witness to the world. He is, as he claims, the "Columbus of those near-at-hand," because he *is* rediscovering America, and *has* found the twentieth-century American equivalents of Caesars, Quixotes, and Pucks. The heroic qualities are not in himself, but in the people he meets in his unteleological roaming. He lives as an aware Aboveground Man. The man aware knows there is limitless fiction in the fall of a sparrow.

Bellow's novella, *Seize the Day* (1956), which followed *Augie March,* shows the courage shown by, say, Joyce, in creating a hero like Leopold Bloom — a hero who is objectively unworthy.

Bellow's Tommy Wilhelm lives at the center of America's contradiction: on one hand we assume that *to be born is to be,* but our day-to-day existence follows the formula *to be is to succeed.* The American Way of Life says *all men are created equal, but only he who rings the bell gets the cigar.* Wilhelm, no bell ringer, is lamenting his denial by the world. America's standard is simple: anybody who can count can measure success. "How much is he worth?" has a double-entry bookkeeping rather than a metaphysical answer. By the money standard Wilhelm is a failure. Society's other standards rule against him: he is no longer a son (his successful old father turns him away), neither husband nor ex-husband (his wife Margaret refuses to make his leaving easy); he is no father, no businessman, no depositor, no spender. Cleaned out, he cries aloud for existential recognition because he is a "man" and "human," nothing more.

Wilhelm is Bellow's victim writ large, with just enough self-awareness to recognize his unheroic nature, his absurdity, his unimportance. Wilhelm's fate puts the question clearly: what does the world promise the untalented, the unsuccessful, the unlovable? Only as the gull of con-man Tamkin has Wilhelm made it. *I am a mark, therefore I am* answers no existential question.

Wilhelm sees himself as griffon-ridden, dragon-harried, vulture-torn, but, mock-Prometheus, he could not sup a starling: "I was the man beneath; Tamkin was on my back, and I thought I was on his. He made me carry him, too, besides Margaret. Like this

15

they ride on me with hoofs and claws. Tear me to pieces, stamp on me and break my bones."

Bellow's legend makes Wilhelm cry, "Help!" in a bored world that hears it as "Wolf!" Wilhelm's last-mile walk ends with him crying in a commercial burial-parlor over the dead body of an unknown man in the company of strangers. The pathos of the objectively unworthy man is a high moment in Bellow's art.

Bellow's free-style *Augie March* language reappears in *Seize the Day* to objectify everything alive and vital and beautiful but missing from Wilhelm's life. The lyric vision of New York City accentuates Wilhelm's bleakness and his loneliness. Bellow has relentlessly brought a hero of the American middle-class world, who knows only how to measure with money, to the point at which there is no money to measure with. His "death of a salesman," unlike Arthur Miller's, blames no vague "somebody," and so does not shift the focus of pain and anguish off that salesman, Wilhelm. Bellow, in a way, has gone beyond Joyce's Bloom with Wilhelm: added to Bloom's impotence and ineptness in a hostile world he has Wilhelm's untalented and unlovable nature. People think Bloom is "a bit of an artist"; Molly loves Bloom in her fashion; Bloom had a loving, if strange father, has had glowing moments with parents, wife, child, job, history — Wilhelm is nothing, has nothing, anticipates nothing. In his fate Bellow has written the meaning of money. Nihilism has a new definition: no money.

In an attempt to break with the givens of his earlier work, Bellow in 1959 left the Jewish, lower or middle middle-class level of his previous fiction and turned to the last shout of a dying American aristocracy. A former anthropology student, Bellow took his new hero, Henderson, away from American sophistication and culture, to a concrete place, Africa, which, because of its weirdness to an American, becomes unreal, outside the press of space, time, and money. Africa allows for the confrontation of man as animal, as evolution, as spirit, rather than as function, statistic, category. Henderson is a recoil from Wilhelm: his question starts from the idea "What if one had plenty of money, and a place in society, and a wife, and children, and some role in history, some claim on tradition, some place in the given world — then what?" Will an affirmative check-mark in all man's questing categories add up to a significant answer — personally and generically — to the riddle of human existence?

Henderson the Rain King is Bellow's Karamazov novel: he tries to move his hero Henderson into situations which, like Dostoevski's, allow for endlessly intricate dialogues. Sporting the familiar Bellow motifs of gums and teeth and noses and knots in the chest, tightnesses in the throat, and assorted stress symptoms, Henderson still manages to leave his aristocratic home, his country's protections, to abandon his own fetishes; in darkest Africa, he confronts ultimate meaning in the flip of a log, a break in a dental bridge, the discovery of a dead body, the talk of a black King, the flight of a plane over water.

The escape clauses for Henderson are numerous: he's a bear, a boor, not his literary father's son. But Bellow in *Henderson the Rain King* attempts fiction which transcends definitions, and, so, escape clauses. One by one Henderson eliminates all the rationales and alibis of birth and upbringing, and talent, which would give him an out, let him "break up his lines to weep." Even his age — 55 — he dismisses as a valid excuse for giving up the quest for change. He leaves America because society can't explain the things that happen to men and women, or offer any calming gift to still the voice in Henderson that cries out, "I want, I want." Henderson can attain much, sustain nothing. His feeling is intense, but evanescent: a flop with his children, he can feel love for a Persian child who will not be around to bug him in the morning. In Africa the emotional life is easy, because unreal. In Africa Henderson's flubbyknuckled blundering is as good a way to make it through the twenty-four-hour day as any other. But throughout his African sojourn Henderson looks for some clue, some carry-home message, some key to his personality or his physiology which will open him to undiscovered worlds.

Henderson the Rain King is a Bergsonian book, a saddened Nietzsche's book, in which Bellow's hero is trying to discover his meaning as evolution before re-entering the *Augie March* world of reality and history to define himself as individual. Bellow's forthcoming novel, *Herzog* (a section of which has already appeared) tries once more, as *Augie March* did, to merge man's double quest for a role in the present and in the history of the race. Herzog touches history by writing letters, real and imaginary, to the greats who "run things." In the name of himself and mankind he is entering a comic Metaphysical Complaint and a Mock-Lamentation against everyone in power and out who has trespassed on Herzog's and man's dignity. Herzog is Bellow's recognizable victim made comic, self-conscious, ironic, tranquilized. The victim as tensioneer has disappeared: his bill of particulars no longer serves to incriminate the universe.

Bellow's career so far, then, is a microcosm of the main developments in his generation's fiction. Themes and ideas which occur in Bellow's novels recur in the work of other serious writers of this period, Ralph Ellison's *Invisible Man* (1952), Norman Mailer's *The Naked and the Dead* (1948), William Styron's *Lie Down in Darkness* (1951), and in the novels of James Baldwin, Bernard Malamud, Flannery O'Connor, among others. But just as Bellow moves ever further from the definitions of his own environment — Jewish, educated, middle class, big city — so each of the writers I've mentioned tends either to escape or to struggle against the limitations of regional, racial, or social definition.

A writer of the 1930's like Richard Wright is a far different "Negro novelist" from Ralph Ellison or James Baldwin. Neither Ellison nor Baldwin has allowed the Negro's color to define his fiction; neither writer has allowed the white society to determine a novel's theme. Ellison writes about Negroes not because they are discriminated against but because he knows them best. He and Baldwin do not create fictions to affirm what the white society denies or deny what the white society affirms. The Negro is one special kind of human being whose equality is a matter of humanity, not merely of Rights. The Negro is as capable of being dehumanized by his friends as by his enemies; Ellison's and Baldwin's freedom to portray the Negro as evil is part of the continuing liberation of the creative imagination in America. Wright wrote about *black* men; Ellison and Baldwin write about black *men* — either feels free to write about white men the way most white novelists feel free to write about black. In the descriptions of the Magi wonder and awe are unaffected by whose skin was dark and whose white.

Unlike Bellow, who, in a more belletristic age might have been an essayist or a writer of nondramatic dialogues, Ralph Ellison is a highly dramatic novelist whose drama forces rather than prepares the way for generalization and reflection. Where Bellow's books are often analogous with the last act of a Shaw play, Ellison's *Invisible Man* (as well as the two parts of his second novel so far published) belongs to a world violent as Kyd's or Webster's, tumultuous as the Ahab universe in *Moby Dick*. Where an Augie March records and discusses, Ellison's nameless hero feels and swings; where Bellow's characters try to take Augie over, make him over, convert him, Ellison's threaten, batter, envelope, gobble up, beat against his hero. Augie tries to learn *how* to live in the world; Ellison's hero has, every day, to prove life possible. And where Augie's past is something he is willing to slough off for the great new wonder, the present, Ellison's hero has his color and his past and character as *given*, to be struggled with and against at the very moment life itself is endangered.

The two parts of *Invisible Man* stand as a symbolic tale of the Negro in America, almost allegories, as it were, of, first, the Negro in the South, and, then, the Negro in the North. Gilding the lily, drawing a mustache on the Mona Lisa, Ellison also plays the popular game of Mythic Parallel, in building into *Invisible Man* a Rhadamanthus legend of the Underworld which, fortunately, does not obscure his massive imagination. His novel cries the Negro's inability to achieve the minimal — human recognition, elusive in the hands of friends *and* enemies. The Negro in America is invisible because he is a "cause" or an "abomination" or a Faulknerian symbol, a black abstraction subject to dehumanization by brutalizing racists or pastoralizing reformers.

Ellison's book reaches beyond the category of "blame." His hero is one of the first Negro characters to insert himself in the roll call of villains. Ultimately, as I've suggested, Ellison is asking for the *equality of evil* which will end invisibility: "I am an invisible man . . . simply because people refuse to see me. . . . When they approach me they see only my surroundings, themselves, or figments of their imagination — indeed, everything and anything except me. . . . You ache with the need to convince yourself that you exist in the real world . . ."

Invisibility is a condition of the North; agony is the condition of the South. Ellison's South is Conrad's heart of darkness, where the Kurtzes of the world lord it over the "natives," secure in their knowledge that no outside force will restrain them. In such a world Ellison's narrator cannot even attain the minimal human definition which would allow for a Huck Finn adventure. His narrator, who wants to make a speech about humility to a "Kurtz Society" smoker, is told he must first take part in a battle royal to be fought by some of his schoolmates "as part of the entertainment." His observation: "I suspected that fighting a battle royal might detract from the dignity of my speech. In those pre-invisible days I visualized myself as a potential Booker T. Washington."

The smoker is an angry swirl of Negro terror and white brutal vulgarity — a naked blonde dancing before "bankers, lawyers, judges, doctors, fire chiefs, teachers, merchants . . . one of the more fashionable pastors"; the battle royal proper; the Negro boys picking coins off an electrified rug: "Suddenly I saw a boy lifted into the air, glistening with sweat like a circus seal, and dropped, his wet back landing flush upon the charged rug, heard him yell and saw him literally dance upon his back, his elbows beating a frenzied tatoo upon the floor, his muscles twitching like the flesh of a horse stung by many flies. When he finally rolled off, his face was gray and no one stopped him when he ran from the floor amid booming laughter." And finally, the speech itself, which, symbolically, the narrator tries to deliver with dignity and purpose while he is being interrupted, laughed at, scolded, warned with the cliché of clichés, "We mean to do right by you, but you've got to know your place at all times."

Ellison's artistic problem becomes the problem of the Negro in a white society: how is it possible to make the white man so aware of the Negro's humanity that he forgets the destiny he is involved with is a black man's? The pilgrimage of the northern white trustee, Norton, to the narrator's college is intended to thrust Norton into a world experienced in its effects and not dwindled away back to causes. The Negro liberated from all forms of economic and political and social humiliation can then know suffering.

Ellison's hero, unsurprisingly, finds new and even greater terrors in the North, a Black Bilbo in Ras the Destroyer, an unsheeted Ku Klux Klan in Harlem's Black Muslims, a world so violent that his way of fending off horror — irony, detachment, amused descriptions of the hopelessness of being Negro — fails him. Which is what makes him "invisible," makes him stay in the hole he has fallen in while eluding Ras's men. All victories in the aboveground world are Pyrrhic for the Negro. The cynic who is Rinehart may imagine himself engaged as a black underground man: Ellison's hero prefers to live his fantasy life literally below ground. He comes up only when he is convinced that his individual destiny is really *not* that important.

Ellison achieves a level of affirmation which transcends the usual heroic acting-out of the "aye." In the midst of his own personal agony the narrator realizes that it is not him but life itself which is to be affirmed, and that its affirmation is unconditional, while man's at best is confused and uncertain: "I condemn and affirm, say no and say yes, say yes and say no."

Just as Bellow's Augie makes a claim for himself as the "Columbus of those near-at-hand," Ellison's narrator offers himself as more representative than unique: "I looked at Ras . . . and recognized the absurdity of the whole night and of the simple yet confoundingly complex arrangement of hope and desire, fear and hate, that had brought me here still running, and knowing now who I was and where I was and knowing too that I had no longer to run for or from the Jacks and the Emersons and the Bledsoes and Nortons, but only from their confusion, impatience, and refusal to recognize the beautiful absurdity of their American identity and mine."

In his epilogue the narrator stakes Ellison's claim that *Invisible Man* is not only representative of America, white and black, but also of twentieth-century man, and, indeed, man in any time, in any place: "Who knows but that, on the lower frequencies, I speak for you?"

In his "And Hickman Arrives" fragment from a second novel,

Ellison has indicated what *Invisible Man* demonstrably asserts: that his may turn out to be the most alive fictional talent of his generation, and perhaps, with Faulkner and Melville and Twain, of American writing of all time. No other writer of this generation, certainly, has Ellison's power of dramatization, his ability to create a scene that is concrete, moving, leaping aesthetic distances to pull the reader into a character's experience. Where Bellow's hero is on a road that might go either right or left without affecting the quality of the novel or the lessons drawn from his action, Ellison's hero moves inevitably, irresistibly, like lava which, once started, flows till the volcano's exhausted. The dramatic texture of Ellison's fiction, *as experience*, does something few American novels of this or any other generation have been able to do — create a world so true to itself that even pedestrianizing journalistic reviewers suspend, if only for the moment, their usual categories of "the believable," "the credible," "the recognizable," "the convincing."

This talent creates myths rather than mythic parallels. Ellison, like Faulkner, casts new scales of life, projects presences free of the usual restrictions imposed by space and time. The reportorial equivalent of the following "And Hickman Arrives" passage would lose the essential life, the style, the rhythm, not only of Ellison but of the South and America. The scene itself is daring and wild — a young boy in a coffin to act out, during a sermon, the meaning of resurrection: "It was not yet time. I could hear the waves of Daddy Hickman's voice rolling against the sides, then down and back, now to boom suddenly in my ears as I felt the weight of darkness leave my eyes, bright air bringing the odor of flowers. I lay there blinking up at the lights, the satin corrugations of the slanting lid and the vague outlines of Deacon Wilhite, who was now moving aside, so that it seemed as though he had himself been the darkness. I lay there deeply inhaling the flowers as I released Teddy's paw and grasped my white Bible with both hands, feeling the chattering and the real terror beginning. . . . Always at the sound of Daddy Hickman's voice I came floating up like a corpse shaken loose from the bottom of a river."

Though Ellison's characters cast mammoth shadows, they are not symbols or vaguenesses who use the space-time world only as raw material out of which to make the higher literary realities. Ellison's Negro world, like Bellow's Jewish world, or Styron's South, Morris's West, Mailer's Army and his California, Malamud's Campus, Algren's Chicago, is a world realized in its concreteness. The aboveground novelist makes of the things of this world a dimension beyond ideology and special pleading: the representation of the visible world becomes an end as well as a generalizing means.

The state of fiction at this time may be inevitable: in its first phase the novel may tell what life here is like; in its second phase it may probe the meaning of life here; in the third phase we are in now, the novel uses the space-time world as a theater of significant action. The region, *fully realized,* is the world: so too a people or a great event.

As the case for man becomes more urgent, the case for a region or a religion or a people tends to sound less urgent: the case for the Negro as Negro, the Jew as Jew, the southerner as southerner has already been made. Where the 1930's and 1940's exposed "the truth" and presented "problems," the 1950's see in every man man's overwhelming questions.

So it is that Norman Mailer's *The Naked and the Dead* (1948) makes of World War II an existential arena for the proving of men and, ultimately, man. Mailer's book is both reportage and dramatic fiction; it is historical in its presentation of the Japanese phase of the war and ahistorical in its dramatization of men in crisis. The inevitable and perhaps necessary theme of "war is hell" is combined with war as the Great Event of Mailer's contemporary experience.

Mailer, whose artistic and intellectual failings are obvious, has still written the best book about the war. What he says of his General Cummings ironically extends to his novel itself: Cummings was "The Professor . . . The General, The Statesman, The Philosopher. . . . Each of these poses had been a baffling mixture of the genuine and the sham" — Mailer, like Salinger, has an embarrassingly uncomfortable fix on the phony.

Mailer's baroque quest leads him to try all styles and all levels of flight: his dialogues, his choruses, his Time Machine sets, his dialects, his debates, his sentimentality, Hemingway tough-guyness, Eliotic abstruseness, work through a multiplicity of points of views and positions in America's many hierarchies. What results is a counterpointed texture of cliché and cynicism, flagwaving and sourness, pragmatism and nihilism, with many targets and snipers-at-targets combined in a weaving prose. His heroic General Cummings sets a text for his Lieutenant Hearn and everybody else to obliterate, " 'The trick is to make yourself an instrument of your own policy . . . the highest effectiveness man has achieved.' " But when Hearn is dead and the General concedes his campaign was a "botch," he has an unheroic Tolstoian vision of war: "For a moment he almost admitted that he had had very little or perhaps nothing at all to do with this victory, or indeed any victory — it had been accomplished by a random play of vulgar good luck larded into a causal net of factors too large, too vague, for him to comprehend. He allowed himself this thought, brought it almost to the point of words and then forced it back. But it caused him a deep depression."

Mailer's feeling about the war and the world is pointed up by the ending of *The Naked and the Dead*: for though the book has

25

been concerned with the dilemmas of a Hamlet, the world is in-herited — as Hamlet himself said it would be — by the book's Osric, Major Dalleson, worrying about how to requisition a photo of Betty Grable.

Mailer's second novel, *Barbary Shore* (1951), is by Bellow's *Dangling Man* out of Hemingway — not the Hemingway of *Fare-well to Arms* who weaves in and out of *The Naked and the Dead,* nor the Hemingway of *The Sun Also Rises* who gives Mailer's third novel, *The Deer Park* (1955), its form and style and tone, but rather the Hemingway of such short stories as "The Killers." The new dimension in Mailer's second novel is politics, or more precisely a socialist vantage point from which to take stock of postwar America. His aspiring writer, Lovett, is, like Sergius O'Shaugnessy of *The Deer Park,* a veteran trying to find his way back into whatever reality the world still has to offer. But the war has to be figured out, analyzed in pseudo-Marxian, mock-Fabian terms, so: "I mulled the history of that first war which ended probably before I was born, and the second which had swallowed me, and the third which was preparing. . . . There had been a heritage but it was given away, and the labor boss, the hack, and the Fabian devoured it among themselves."

What follows is a debate between Hollingsworth, the new man, and McLeod who wants to retreat from politics back to his gross wife, Guinevere, and forget his part in the Cause that destroyed Leon Trotsky. McLeod's confession to Lovett is a confession of political senselessness: " 'I let him be killed because I hated him, because the thought that all through the years with all his theo-retical bilge about a degenerated workers' state, he was still nearer the truth than I had been, and my life was the lie, and the thought of him was unbearable for he had a knack to activate the tumor in all of us until it gave no rest . . .' "

Barbary Shore switches styles and levels from page to page, ending with the slaughter of McLeod, and Lovett's Jeremiah vision of the world's inevitable destruction: "Meanwhile, vast armies mount themselves, the world revolves, the traveller clutches his breast. From out the unyielding contradictions of labor stolen from men, the march to the endless war forces its pace. Perhaps, as the millions will be lost, others will be created, and I shall discover brothers where I thought none existed. But for the present the storm approaches its thunderhead, and it is apparent that the boat drifts ever closer to shore. So the blind will lead the blind, and the deaf shout warnings to one another until their voices are lost."

The Deer Park is post-Korea and thus free of *Barbary Shore*'s fear of a dreaded third world war. The excesses and bad taste of Mailer's first two novels turn up again in a kind of *roman à clef* about the film world, a 1950's remake of *The Sun Also Rises*. Much of the book sounds like dialogue spun out of "Dear Abby" columns, boring but justifiable as an accurate version of that peculiar Far West dramatization of the Decline of the West. Mailer is always writing about something Big: the Big War; the Big Political Threat; the Big Glamour Industry; and the Big Sellout — the world and theme of *The Deer Park.*

The Deer Park has much to say about the Affairs-of-Men-and-Women, much about Career-and-Compromise, something about the nastiness of the House Un-American Activities Committee in Hollywood. But the zing of an *Augie March* and the broad span of *Invisible Man* and the moral fervor and intellectual intensity of *The Naked and the Dead* are missing: Mailer has not found a way of raising the cliché to the level of art — as, say, Joyce has in *Ulysses* and *Finnegans Wake*; the result is a novel that is itself a cliché.

Yet, Mailer's failures, like his heroic attempts, work on a vast scale: his sometimes messy prose and his sometimes fatuous generalizations belong to that baroque attempt to grasp all. Though he lacks the neatness and muted good taste of a Salinger or an Updike, his striving for ultimates, if not his success in achieving them, makes him a close relation of strivers like Bellow and Ellison and Styron.

J. D. Salinger, of course, writes far neater books, and for far neater audiences. Salinger's fiction is in tune with the urbanity and sophistication of the *New Yorker*'s talk-of-the-town pieces, its gentlemanly, not-too-professional inquiry into science and contemporary personalities, its wry cartoons, its up-to-the-minute stylishness in dress, drink, and vacation. His Christian symbolism is recognizable and unfervid, his Zen properly unshrill.

Salinger's *The Catcher in the Rye* (1951), to date his only novel (though one might make the different sections of the Glass family legend a novel), is an interesting departure from its model, *The Adventures of Huckleberry Finn*. Where Twain's Huck is one who looks at the world in a special way, Salinger's Holden Caulfield is one who is tagged and labeled inside and out in order to appear as imaginatively realized as Huck. Holden's experience of the contemporary world is restricted to what a nice prep school boy should know — teachers, parents of fellow students, taxi drivers, elevator operators — with just enough variation (nuns, prostitutes) to mark himself *New Yorker* bizarre, and odd-ball. Holden is compounded of crutches of style, tags, and expletives which are supposed to suggest a seventeen-year-old mind has been successfully created: Holden is not seventeen because he looks at the world with a seventeen-year-old's eye, but because he uses words like "goddam," "hell," "crap," "boring," "mad," "depressing," "phony," while, at the same time, with a secret heart of gold, feels sorry for the people he despises. He feels *real* love for his sister Phoebe, his dead brother Allie, his Hollywood-writer brother D. B. Like the Glasses of *Franny and Zooey* (1961), Holden belongs to a family world where communion, understanding, and loyalty *are* possible but set off from the crumby world outside, where "People are always ruining things for you."

The Caulfields, like the Glasses, are violets in a world of mossy stones. They are *mad* and *crazy* because of their fine sensitivity and their separation from reality's slobs, boors, phonies, and activists. Holden makes much of being "yellow," which is a sign of his feeling, his sensitivity to pain, loss, fear, and humiliation: the *un*yellow are the unfeeling. This is the code of the Glass menagerie, where fear and crack-up and even death are proofs of the soul's existence, demonstrations of uninstitutionalized religious *un*phoniness; the unphony Christ if differentiated from phony Christians and all other unnice phonies who make the Caulfields and the Glasses crowd together like last survivors in the universe's spiritual fallout shelter.

As one reads *The Catcher in the Rye* one wonders constantly what Holden would do were Salinger to produce not a cliché Chippsian character he can patronize, like old Spencer, and not a cliché parent like Mrs. Morrow, nor a cliché instructor like Mr. Antolini. Huck Finn constantly makes the world more than it is, using either his fantasies or his imagination. The world Holden Caulfield encounters is one of categories: apart from his references to Christ in upper-case reverence, and his apparently shocking language, his range of experience is the researched and authenticated reality sophisticated magazines have inculcated in their regulars. Huck is a hero-worshiper and myth-maker who constantly overcomes the shoddiness of the world's givens. The often ironic texture of *Huckleberry Finn* comes from the gap between Huck's admiring view and the cynical view of the reader. In Salinger's work, unfortunately, the irony may be produced by the reader wondering if Holden and Seymour and Zooey and Buddy admire *enough.*

Holden's New York is no surprise and no wonder, as Huck's River is: his city is the one approved for college weekends, complete with the whispers and side excursions promised in prep school locker rooms.

Reading *The Catcher in the Rye* one wonders if Salinger might ever produce a character on the level of the ones he and his characters admire so *in literature*. Does the lack in this twentieth century of a Zossima or an Ivan Karamazov or a Hamlet justify the attitudes and isolation of the Caulfields and the Glasses? Is Salinger's paper world of "phonies" gratuitously produced to prove the Caulfields and the Glasses *right?* Their pantheon is peopled by the dead unphony — writers, figures out of history and literature, fictional characters in Salinger's hierarchy. One thinks, rather pointedly, of a Caulfield or a Glass confronted not by an easy mark like Spencer but by an Einstein, and wonders, again, whether the reiteration of the phony in Salinger's work is not a willed denial of a possibility the fictions are incapable of producing. To people the world with shams in order to conclude it is full of shams is, after all, artistic dirty pool.

Salinger's debt in *The Catcher in the Rye* to *Huckleberry Finn* indicates the importance of Mark Twain to American fiction of the post-World War II period, which, however, is still as committed as it ever was to Melville, and *Moby Dick. Moby Dick* is the Big American Novel which, magnificent in its parts, breaks down as a realized artistic whole but yet rises to the greatest heights imaginable in prose literature. In the continuing Big Novel tradition of the South *Moby Dick* is most celebrated.

The South has seen the novel flower in the twentieth century in Faulkner's *The Sound and the Fury, Absalom! Absalom!, Light in August,* and in the books of Robert Penn Warren, Carson McCullers, Eudora Welty, and, most recently, Katherine Anne Porter. In this generation we are considering, the South is represented by Truman Capote, Flannery O'Connor, and, most impressively, by its current continuator of the *Moby Dick* tradition, William Styron.

Like Bellow, Ellison, and Mailer, Styron produces great writing but not necessarily great books. He and Capote both recognize the South as a particular place which, realized fully, speaks itself and more than itself. They do not turn their backs on the South as a "region," but they are not regional writers. Styron has said, "I would like to believe that my people would have behaved the way they did anywhere."

Styron's work, in fact, is consciously European. He is also the most self-consciously "literary" of this generation's novelists. His characters can usually take part in college bull-sessions directed to the Big Questions about literature American and Comparative, about philosophy Ancient and Modern. Styron's awareness makes his fiction complex and double: his characters strive for meaning in a world of *un*meaning. They contemplate that *un*meaning as man's doomed, though perhaps heroic, attempt to overcome the absurd and fashion himself a dignified fate.

His first novel, *Lie Down in Darkness* (1951), is a southern version of Mann's *Doctor Faustus* and Mann's *Buddenbrooks*, which switches from microcosm to macrocosm, from a man's individual fate to man's historical destiny; characters act out the destructive force of history and, at other times, history expresses the destructive force of men. The form of the book is significant, framed by suicide and burial, built on a funereal procession. Styron's dead heroine, Peyton Loftis, is not the powerful and ironically triumphant Addie Bundren of Faulkner's *As I Lay Dying*, whose force and defeat dominates each of the book's interior monologues. *Lie Down in Darkness* lacks such a center, and so turns into a *Ulysses* without a Stephen or Bloom, a *Ring and the Book* with no other point to make than that man's search for elusive reality will end only in his discovering an unbearable record of human destruction.

Peyton Loftis is not Freud's but a Greek tragedian's Electra: her mother, Helen — a grown-old destroyer of not-so-noble Trojans — is not only the predictable Clytemnestra of the Electra triangle but also a female Creon brought face to face with the senselessness of a child's death. Recognition, in Styron's work, does not lead to peace or resolution. Both Helen and her husband Milton see in their recognition only horror.

Styron's theme sometimes seems little different from the standard Beat lament; but his fiction also contains a relieving glimpse of a southern *style* that once was, and a human *joy* that might be. In the midst of the Loftis turmoil, a norm, Peyton's Harry, calls the world to witness the foolishness of human wishes and petty evil in a new universe exploded into being by the bomb at Hiroshima. In the scale of *this* destructiveness man's own destructiveness seems paltry, irrelevant, absurd.

After a small book, *The Long March* (1952), a kind of existential exercise, Styron in 1960 published a sprawl of a novel, *Set This House on Fire*, a book intended — one hopes — to objectify in its chaotic, arbitrary, unfinished, undramatized, uncentered form the presence of these qualities in twentieth-century experience. The book is a prose *La Dolce Vita*, a Thomas Wolfe tome that shifts point of view variously and unnecessarily, packs in long *Esquire*-cum-Hollywood up-to-the-second chitchat about higher things. *Set This House on Fire* is on location in Italy, a twentieth-century American-in-Italy analogue of James's nineteenth-century American-in-Paris. Styron's characters ride an inflationary wave Fitzgerald's people knew in pre-crash Paris. Peter Leverett, narrator of the book's opening, is, as a character, less important than Cass Kinsolving, narrator of the central action — Cass's murdering of Mason Flagg.

Out of the unrealized legends and actions of the novel Styron does manage to construct a significant tale of Mason Flagg, his meaning as evil, violence, guilt, and redemption. The wildness of the Italian world allows full indulgence to Styron's credo of "When in doubt turn on the prose."

Mason Flagg is a great malignant, a colder Don Giovanni and righteous Judas whose death Styron meticulously delineates. Cass Kinsolving is a fine portrait of a destroyed man brought back to life by love, and horror at the abomination, Flagg. Kinsolving kills as Mann's Mario in *Mario and the Magician* kills — because the last sign of human dignity is suddenly assailed by Flagg. He kills because he sees a choice between "nothingness and being," which even weekend existentialists have little difficulty differentiating. But his facing down of evil doesn't lead to understanding: as he tells Peter Leverett: " 'Not too long ago . . . they'd hang a ten-year-old for stealing a nickel's worth of candy. . . . This was the plague theory . . . Now a kid . . . commits . . . murder maybe, and they call him sick . . . on the theory that the evil is . . . a temporary resident in the brain. And both of these theories are as evil as the evil they are intended to destroy and cure. . . . Yet for the life of me I don't know of any nice golden mean between the two.' "

Styron's fascination with evil is seen in other southern writers of this generation, such as Truman Capote. Like Styron, who is equally fascinated by destroyers who are "bright" and "fun" and great to get drunk with, Capote consistently leans on what he would put down. Like Styron he frequently is "amusing" and "entertaining" with characters and actions he has judged and found wanting. His first novel, *Other Voices, Other Rooms* (1948), is another American book in the Huck Finn line, but with significant Capote alterations. Everything in his world is turned two or three degrees off plumb. If Holden Caulfield's adventure in

New York suffers from being predictable, Joel Knox's in Noon City suffers equally from *not* being so. Capote's Randolph and his weirdos of Skully's Landing are of a characteristic oddness and grotesqueness. Styron in doubt turns on the prose; Capote turns on the poetry. His Joel's consciousness turns lyric and takes on an undramatic life of its own.

Capote's tremblingly poetic style frequently pre-empts the matter of fiction, as this concluding cadence from *Other Voices, Other Rooms* indicates: "A sound, as if the bell had suddenly tolled, and the shape of loneliness, greenly iridescent, whitely indefinite, seemed to rise from the garden . . . Gradually the blinding sunset . . . darkened, and it was as if snow were falling there, flakes shaping snow-eyes, hair: a face trembled like a white beautiful moth, smiled. She beckoned to him, shining and silver, and he knew he must go . . ."

Styron's novels are peopled by well-heeled, beer-guzzling, suddenly idea-stricken "Gentleman C" party boys who use their college education rather well; Capote's books teem with the poetic isolate, the *"figure pâle"* of French nineteenth-century verse and prose, the tremulous and petal-conscious young men of the disestablishment.

In his second short novel, *The Grass Harp* (1951), Capote once more delineated the southern world set, like an awry pinball machine, permanently at "Tilt." Reality is seen from a treehouse where five characters take refuge from mock representations of the religious and civil powers in their world. The treehouse becomes a kind of ark during the world's deluge of madness, and Capote suggests that when his central character, Collin, and the others finally come down from the tree, their stay there, like Noah's on the ark and Huck's on the raft, increases their power to deal with the real world.

Capote's heroine of his third novel, *Breakfast at Tiffany's*

(1958), Holly Golightly, describes the quality of his early fiction crudely but significantly: " 'Brats and niggers. Trembling leaves. *Description*. It doesn't *mean* anything.' " Holly, on the other hand, is Capote's breakthrough character, an amoral ingénue with great style and vitality *and* meaning, artistically a success. She is superficiality humanized. Capote in Holly has successfully bypassed the cliché of satire. He has "exposed" the Hollywood gossip column–midtown Manhattan bar world without denying the Hollys of that world their human dimension. The Salinger phony has been replaced by a " *'real* phony,' " as O. J. Berman, Hollywood, U.S.A., has it. In the midst of madness and three-dollar bills Holly pushes toward recognition, a meaning to transcend the lunacy of her activities and the people around her: " 'If I were free to choose from everybody alive, just snap my fingers and say come here you, I wouldn't pick José. Nehru, he's nearer the mark. Wendell Willkie. I'd settle for Garbo any day. Why not? A person ought to be able to marry men or women or — listen, if you came to me and said you wanted to hitch up with Man o' War, I'd respect your feeling. No, I'm serious. Love should be allowed.' "

Holly's life sums up the unreality of the gay life in America. She involves herself with the Mafia, films, international lovers, the 400, penniless writers (like the novel's narrator), dope, whisky, but, like a true southern heroine (Texas belle that she is), continues to love her elderly husband, Doc, her brother (whose death shivers her unreality), her cat. Capote, like Salinger, creates anti-characters, for Holly one Mildred Grossman: "Mildred: with her moist hair and greasy spectacles, her stained fingers that dissected frogs and carried coffee to picket lines, her flat eyes that turned toward the stars to estimate their chemical tonnage. . . . Earth and air could not be more opposite than Mildred and Holly, yet in my head they acquired a Siamese twinship, and the thread of thought that had sewn them together ran like this: the average personality reshapes frequently . . . desirable or not, it is a natural thing that we should change. All right, here were two people who never would . . . the one had splurged herself into a top-heavy realist, the other a lopsided romantic."

Capote, of course, has thrown in his lot with the "lopsided romantic." Let the saviors of the world beware lest they get grease on their spectacles or stains on their fingers! Holly is a woman with *clean* hair and *clear* glasses and a code: "'I may be rotten to the core, Maude, *but*: testify against a friend I will not. Not if they can prove he doped Sister Kenny.'"

Holly sums up American confusion: in her hour of need, all she wants is her St. Christopher medal — bought at Tiffany's. As she's jumping bail she abandons her cat and suddenly *sees*: "'I'm very scared, Buster. Yes, at last. Because it could go on forever. Not knowing what's yours until you've thrown it away.'"

Stylistically, Holly is important too, and southern. Southern writers use pitchmen's and Biblical rhythms as a kind of music in reserve. Ordinary discourse and narrative, particularly that form which derives from Hemingway, is neither incantatory nor lyrical; the contemporary novelist is attracted to characters like Holly who are unlimited and uninhibited *stylistically* — Irish and Welsh bards, Yiddish mammas, Negro preachers, carnival pitchmen, conmen, blue-tongued monologists like this same Holly. The conformity of character and manners in the twentieth century has its equivalent in the colorlessness and predictability of contemporary talk and rhythm. The writer of this generation breaks through into unique rhythms by creating unique characters like Holly.

Styron's Daddy Faith of *Set This House on Fire*, and Dolly of Capote's *The Grass Harp*, have that desired Biblical and lyric dimension. In Flannery O'Connor's fiction Biblical texture becomes the matter of an entire novel. Her first book, *Wise Blood* (1952), reverberates with wild Christian preaching. The Bible, *as style*, becomes the objective correlative for uniqueness, individuation, and the passionate commitment (even of the mad and the fanatic) elsewhere absent in the contemporary world. *Wise Blood* is grotesque to avoid being lukewarm.

Miss O'Connor neither misrepresents nor even, perhaps, exaggerates reality: she merely closes the sky in over Haze Motes and Enoch Emory so that no norm exists to measure their fanaticism by. Haze denounces Christ and imitates Christ, preaches the gospel of the "Church without Christ" as a furious text. But reality could be so deadened to Christ's word that nothing less than a Haze may awaken it. Or weird Enoch with his embalmed, shrunken "jesus" and his own "revelation" in a gorilla suit.

The book's ironic ending overcomes the grotesque: self-blinded and self-tortured Haze, dead, is transformed into "back rent" and, in a mock-crucifixion (which doesn't eliminate serious application to the Crucifixion), is delivered to his worldly landlady. Miss O'Connor doesn't transform the landlady but does allow one fast fading glimpse of what Haze's life and Haze's death mean.

In her second novel, *The Violent Bear It Away* (1960), Miss O'Connor discovers what Bellow and Ellison discovered before her: that man's most serious side, contemplated for long, yields to some form of the comic. *The Violent Bear It Away* picks up, in young Tarwater and everyone around him, Haze's extreme fanaticism, but softens the grotesque with humor. To the familiar category of the *repulsively horrifying* one adds the *amusingly absurd*.

That fierce southern revivalist world is found once more in James Baldwin's *Go Tell It on the Mountain* (1953). It *informs* the novel. The Bible represents prose's resistance movement against the flattening tendencies in twentieth-century writing —

Time's anonymous style, nameless but unchangeable because successful; journalistic and academic dullness or turgidity; television and radio commercials; public relations narratives and canned releases. The Bible is a readily available style totally different from ordinary speech not only in rhythm but also in substance. To "turn on the prose" in the South means, usually, to speak with the voice of the prophets. Baldwin's novel does so through Gabriel Grimes: "So he fled from these people, and from these silent witnesses, to tarry and preach elsewhere – to do . . . in secret, his first works over, seeking again the holy fire that had so transformed him once. But he was to find, as the prophets had found, that the whole earth became a prison for him who fled before the Lord. . . . No: though his name was writ large on placards, though they praised him for the great work God worked through him, and though they came . . . before him to the altar, there was no word in the Book for him."

Baldwin, like Styron in *Set This House on Fire* and Capote in *Breakfast at Tiffany's*, who deliberately turned away from the South (perhaps in fear of becoming nothing more than a southern regional writer), in his second novel, *Giovanni's Room* (1956), not only abandoned the South but the world of Negro and white men. In his latest novel, *Another Country* (1962), Baldwin is trying, it seems, to connect the Negro's world with the world in trouble about things other than color.

Change, already observed in Bellow's work, seems to have something inevitable about it: the ambitious American writer fears not only being identified with but being permanently fixed in a region or a cause. So Wright Morris, a "western and midwestern" writer will turn to Europe or Hollywood (which, as everyone knows, is *on* and not *in* the West); Herbert Gold will leave the plastic-sheathed furniture of middle-class Jewish life and write about carnival characters; Harvey Swados will turn aside from the industrial struggle in America and satirize Art living off the Foundations. A similar progression is observable in the work of Bernard Malamud, like Bellow (but unlike Salinger and even Gold) a celebrator of the Jew in America.

Malamud's first novel, *The Natural* (1952), is a baseball book with a difference. Though Malamud, like a good Brooklyn boy, knows baseball and is proud of his baseballmanship, the book uses the baseball world to represent larger human issues. Malamud's second novel, *The Assistant* (1957), makes the life of the Bober family in a tiny backbreaking grocery store the locus for a dramatic action with the categorical complexity of a saint's legend. Malamud counts each Bober day a push on the Sisyphean stone; each Bober reading of the cash register (during the Depression) becomes a trial run for the Day of Judgment.

The Assistant makes interesting contrast with the work of, say, James Farrell or John Steinbeck or the early Dos Passos: in fiction of the thirties, the Depression is an economic and political fact. In Malamud the Depression is but one more manifestation of Jewish, human, agony. Malamud's treatment of the Jewish people of his story also marks a significant change from the fiction of the thirties: discrimination is not important (if it counts at all, Frank Alpine, the Christian, suffers it). Nor is local color. Malamud's focus is on a Bober's burial-before-death existence which, in the middle of New York, ignores New York and is ignored *by* New York. Bober's life seems to make no sense and to lack all hope. Frank Alpine's recognition of Bober enduring, and thus prevailing, does make sense, as his remorse does and his violent affirmation.

Malamud's third novel, *A New Life* (1962), is, almost inevitably, a campus novel, about one S. (Seymour) Levin, a Bellow victim-character, teacher of English at Cascadia College (enrollment, 4200). Levin resembles Herzog, the hero of Bellow's forth-

39

coming novel, but differs in one very important respect: Malamud, unlike Bellow, is still confined by the fictional world he projects for his action. Bellow, as mentioned before, with *Herzog* is trying to break through to the world of politics and history and great decisions. S. Levin's campus, unfortunately, is the campus of American fiction — same-time-same-station — a more human *Groves of Academe* revisited.

S. Levin, however, is no ordinary character, and so long as Malamud sticks with him and avoids the usual satiric targets on a campus, the novel is at its best. Levin is the academe with a sexual fix, a fine comic character who, like Joyce's Leopold Bloom, retains the seriousness of his quest in spite of his obvious inadequacies as a hero. He is an ex-alcoholic in search of a new life, and that new life is a life of love, something his sexual games — at the beginning of the book — lack completely: "Desire butchered him. He beheld his slaughtered face in the mirror and stared at it, wretched. How escape the ferocious lust that enflamed and tormented his thoughts as it corroded his will? . . . Why obsessively seek what was lost — unlived — in the past? He had no wish to be Faust, or Gatsby; or St. Anthony of Somewhere . . . Levin wanted to be himself, at peace in present time."

Levin has experienced Buber's *teshuvah* — a turning — which starts his search for the new life: " 'I was mourning myself. I became a drunk . . . But one morning in somebody's filthy cellar, I awoke under burlap bags and saw my rotting shoes . . . lit in dim sunlight from a shaft or window. . . . Then I thought, Levin, if you were dead there would be no light on your shoes in this cellar. I came to believe what I often wanted to, that life is holy.' "

Levin's final recognition is that it is not necessarily one's own life that is holy but "love of life, anybody's life." Morally, he concludes, he must give up his colleague's wife, Pauline, with whom he has finally "made it" in life. But Levin does *not* give up Pauline. The novel ends with Levin jobless, Pauline pregnant, his car loaded with her adopted children received in trade for his vow to give up college teaching ("you're a fanatical type," Pauline's husband tells Levin). An absurd but at the same time pathetic and heroic ending, not quite so grotesque as Frank Alpine's self-circumcision at the end of *The Assistant,* but at least as ambiguous.

Love, or the lack of it, is the dominant theme of this generation's fiction. Disaffected man contemplates the lack of love — of self, of man, of calling, of the world, of God. Affirmation, when it occurs, is, at best, the tentative, whispered "aye" of Malamud's *A New Life,* or the consciously equivocal "yes" and "no" of *Invisible Man.* In Wright Morris's *Love among the Cannibals* (1957) a middle-aged lover finds himself an "interesting" and necessary "stage" in his young lover-girl's development. In John Updike's second novel, *Rabbit, Run* (1960), his hero Harry Angstrom experiences ample but joyless sexual rapport with his Ruth, and the result is no end to his life's futile drabness.

As in Capote's *Other Voices, Other Rooms* and Baldwin's *Giovanni's Room,* homosexuality as a form of communion emerges from the new American Courtly Love tradition, albeit grotesquely, in James Purdy's *Malcolm* (1959) and his *The Nephew* (1960). In *Malcolm* an inversion of the *Huckleberry Finn* action occurs and the hero, a fifteen-year-old stand-in for Tadzio in Mann's "Death in Venice," embarks on a weird farcical adventure under the aegis of an astrologer called Cox. *The Nephew,* a vengeance on the middle class and its sentimental respectability, tells of a doting aunt and uncle who unfortunately decide to write a memoir of their mysterious, and missing, nephew, Cliff.

What one says about a form that is weekly, daily, being used and fulfilled is, of course, tentative; the writers assayed here are still fairly young, still at work, and capable of great changes, new directions, and fictional surprises. The Aboveground Man emphasis on action and contact with historical reality has, I again suggest, lessened the importance of technical innovation to this generation. Many more writers might have been introduced at any point in the discussion — James Jones and his *From Here to Eternity* (1951) as a companion to Mailer, and, with it, a fine first novel on the POW's in Korea, Francis Pollini's *Night* (1961); George P. Elliott's *Parktilden Village* (1958) and *Among the Dangs* (1961), and Herbert Gold's work, during our consideration of Malamud; Shirley Ann Grau as another side of the South seen by Flannery O'Connor; Nelson Algren as the wilder Chicago version of Saul Bellow; and so on. I should also point out what's obvious, that many of the writers excluded from this study because of prior treatment or other (usually chronological) considerations produced some of their best work during the post-World War II period — Faulkner, Robert Penn Warren, Carson McCullers, Eudora Welty, Ernest Hemingway.

The novel is not dead. Nor is it moribund. Bellow, Ellison, and, on other levels, Styron, Mailer, Baldwin, Capote, Flannery O'Connor, Bernard Malamud, testify that the novel at this time is the American literary form most alive, and thriving. The great desire now is to rejoin the mainstream of the novel of tradition, and, in the space-time world, to re-engage the realities of politics and history. The desire, so far, probably has outdistanced the accomplishment. The Aboveground Man is a greater possibility than he is a realization. But the novel has broken through, and broken out. Liberated from the tyranny of symbolic smallness it has attempted to become *the* literary form to catch the visible world in all its complexity, clangor, and untriumphant celebration. Our times have a tonality the novel cannot ignore.

Selected Bibliography

PRICES are given only for paperback editions, either original or reprint.

Novels

Algren, Nelson. *Never Come Morning.* New York: Harper, 1942.
________. *The Man with the Golden Arm.* Garden City, New York: Doubleday, 1949 (Pocket Books, $.35).
________. *A Walk on the Wild Side.* New York: Farrar, Straus, 1956 (Crest, $.50).
Baldwin, James. *Go Tell It on the Mountain.* New York: Knopf, 1953 (Universal, $1.45).
________. *Notes of a Native Son.* Boston: Beacon, 1955 ($1.25).
________. *Giovanni's Room.* New York: Dial, 1956 (New American Library, $.35).
________. *Another Country.* New York: Dial, 1962.
Bellow, Saul. *Dangling Man.* New York: Vanguard, 1944 (Meridian, $1.25).
________. *The Victim.* New York: Vanguard, 1947 (Compass, $1.25).
________. *The Adventures of Augie March.* New York: Viking, 1953 (Compass, $1.75).
________. *Seize the Day.* New York: Viking, 1956 (Popular Library, $.50).
________. *Henderson the Rain King.* New York: Viking, 1959 (Popular Library, $.50).
Capote, Truman. *Other Voices, Other Rooms.* New York: Random House, 1948 (New American Library, $.35).
________. *The Grass Harp.* New York: Random House, 1951 (New American Library, $.50).
________. *Breakfast at Tiffany's.* New York: Random House, 1958 (New American Library, $.50).
Cheever, John. *Wapshot Chronicle.* New York: Harper, 1957 (Bantam, $.50).
Elliott, George P. *Parktilden Village.* Boston: Beacon, 1958 (Signet Books, $.50).
________. *Among the Dangs.* New York: Holt, Rinehart, and Winston, 1961.
Ellison, Ralph. *Invisible Man.* New York: Random House, 1952 (New American Library, $.75).
Gold, Herbert. *The Birth of a Hero.* New York: Viking Press, 1951.
________. *The Prospect before Us.* Cleveland: World, 1954.

————. *The Man Who Was Not with It.* Boston: Little, Brown, 1956 (Permabooks, $.25).

————. *The Optimist.* Boston: Atlantic-Little, Brown, 1959.

————. *Therefore Be Bold.* New York: Dial, 1960.

Grau, Shirley Ann. *Hard Blue Sky.* New York: Knopf, 1958 (New American Library, $.75).

Holmes, John Clellan. *Go.* New York: Scribner's, 1952 (Ace, $.35).

————. *The Horn.* New York: Random House, 1958 (Crest, $.35).

Jones, James. *From Here to Eternity.* New York: Scribner's, 1951 (Signet, $.95).

————. *Some Came Running.* New York: Scribner's, 1957 (New American Library, $.75).

————. *The Pistol.* New York: Scribner's, 1959 (New American Library, $.50).

Kerouac, Jack. *Town and the City.* New York: Harcourt, Brace, 1950 (Universal, $1.45).

————. *On the Road.* New York: Viking, 1957 (New American Library, $.50).

————. *Dharma Bums.* New York: Viking, 1958 (New American Library, $.50).

————. *Subterraneans.* New York: Evergreen (Grove), 1958 ($1.45).

————. *Doctor Sax.* New York: Evergreen, 1959 ($.75).

————. *Maggie Cassidy.* New York: Avon, 1959 ($.50).

————. *Mexico City Blues: 242 Choruses.* New York: Evergreen, 1959 ($1.95).

————. *Book of Dreams.* San Francisco: City Lights Books, 1961 ($2.50).

Macauley, Robie. *Disguises of Love.* New York: Random House, 1952.

————. *End of Pity.* New York: McDowell, Oblensky, 1957.

Mailer, Norman. *The Naked and the Dead.* New York: Rinehart, 1948 (New American Library, $.50).

————. *Barbary Shore.* New York: Rinehart, 1951 (New American Library, $.50).

————. *The Deer Park.* New York: Putnam, 1955 (New American Library, $.50).

————. *Advertisements for Myself.* New York: Putnam, 1959.

Malamud, Bernard. *The Natural.* New York: Harcourt, Brace, 1952 (Noonday, $1.65).

————. *The Assistant.* New York: Farrar, Straus, 1957 (New American Library, $.50).

————. *Magic Barrel.* New York: Farrar, Straus, 1958 (Vintage, $.95).

————. *A New Life.* New York: Farrar, Straus, 1962.

Morris, Wright. *My Uncle Dudley*. New York: Harcourt, Brace, 1942.

_____. *Man and Boy*. New York: Knopf, 1951.

_____. *The Works of Love*. New York: Knopf, 1952.

_____. *The Deep Sleep*. New York: Scribner's, 1953.

_____. *The Huge Season*. New York: Viking, 1954.

_____. *The Field of Vision*. New York: Harcourt, Brace, 1956 (New American Library, $.50).

_____. *Love among the Cannibals*. New York: Harcourt, Brace, 1957 (New American Library, $.35).

_____. *The Territory Ahead*. New York: Harcourt, Brace, 1958.

_____. *Ceremony in Lone Tree*. New York: Atheneum, 1960.

Nemerov, Howard. *Federigo or the Power of Love*. Boston: Little, Brown, 1954.

_____. *Homecoming Game*. New York: Simon and Schuster, 1957 (Avon, $.35).

O'Connor, Flannery. *Wise Blood*. New York: Harcourt, Brace, 1952.

_____. *The Violent Bear It Away*. New York: Farrar, Straus, 1960 (Signet, $.50).

Pollini, Francis. *Night*. Boston: Houghton Mifflin, 1961.

Purdy, James. *63: Dream Palace* (novella) in *Color of Darkness*. Norfolk, Conn.: New Directions, 1957.

_____. *Malcolm*. New York: Farrar, Straus, 1959.

_____. *The Nephew*. New York: Farrar, Straus, 1960.

Salinger, J. D. *The Catcher in the Rye*. Boston: Little, Brown, 1951 (New American Library, $.50).

_____. "Franny," *New Yorker*, January 29, 1955.

_____. "Zooey," *New Yorker*, May 4, 1957.

_____. "Seymour: An Introduction," *New Yorker*, June 6, 1959.

Stafford, Jean. *Boston Adventure*. New York: Harcourt, Brace, 1944 (Dell, $.75).

Styron, William. *Lie Down in Darkness*. Indianapolis: Bobbs-Merrill, 1951 (New American Library, $.75).

_____. *The Long March*. New York: Random House, 1952 (Vintage, $.95).

_____. *Set This House on Fire*. New York: Random House, 1960 (Signet, $.95).

Swados, Harvey. *Out Went the Candle*. New York: Viking, 1955.

_____. *On the Line*. Boston: Little, Brown, 1957 (Bantam, $.35).

_____. *False Coin*. Boston: Atlantic-Little, Brown, 1959.

_____. *Nights in the Gardens of Brooklyn*. Boston: Atlantic-Little, Brown, 1960.

45

Updike, John. *The Poorhouse Fair*. New York: Knopf, 1959.
_____. *Rabbit, Run*. New York: Knopf, 1960 (Crest, $.50).

Criticism

Aldridge, J. W. *In Search of Heresy*. New York: McGraw-Hill, 1956.
Blair, Walter, and others. *The Literature of the United States*. New York: Scott Foresman, 1957.
Breit, H. *Writer Observed*. Cleveland: World, 1956.
Brossard, Chandler. *The Scene before You*. New York: Rinehart, 1955.
Chase, Richard. *The American Novel and Its Tradition*. Garden City, N.Y.: Doubleday, 1957.
_____. *The Democratic Vista*. Garden City, N.Y.: Doubleday, 1958.
Cowley, Malcolm. *The Literary Situation*. New York: Viking, 1954.
Davidson, Donald. *Southern Writers in the Modern World*. Athens: University of Georgia Press, 1958.
Fiedelson, C. *Interpretations of American Literature*. New York: Oxford University Press, 1959.
Fiedler, Leslie. *End to Innocence*. Boston: Beacon, 1955.
_____. *Love and Death in the American Novel*. New York: Criterion, 1959.
_____. *No! in Thunder*. Boston: Beacon, 1960.
Fischer, John, and Robert Silvers. *Writing in America*. New Brunswick, N.J.: Rutgers University Press, 1960.
Frohock, W. M. *The Novel of Violence in America*. Dallas: Southern Methodist University Press, 1957.
Fuller, Edmund. *Man in Modern Fiction*. New York: Random House, 1958.
Gardiner, Harold C. *In All Conscience*. Garden City, N.Y.: Doubleday, 1959.
Gartenberg, Max, and Gene Feldman. *The Beat Generation and the Angry Young Men*. New York: Citadel, 1958 (Dell, $.50).
Geismar, M. *American Moderns*. New York: Hill and Wang, 1958.
Hassan, Ihab. *Radical Innocence*. Princeton, N.J.: Princeton University Press, 1961.
Hicks, Granville. *The Living Novel*. New York: Macmillan, 1957.
Howard, Leon. *Literature and the American Tradition*. Garden City, N.Y.: Doubleday, 1960.
Howe, Irving. *Politics and the Novel*. New York: Horizon, 1957.
Kazin, Alfred. *Inmost Leaf*. New York: Harcourt, Brace, 1955.
Kenner, Hugh. *Gnomon*. New York: McDowell, Oblensky, 1958.
Leary, Lewis, ed. *Contemporary Literary Scholarship*. New York: Appleton-Century-Crofts, 1958.

————. *American Literary Essays.* New York: Crowell, 1960.

Lipton, Lawrence. *The Holy Barbarians.* New York: Messner, 1959.

Parkinson, Thomas Francis. *A Casebook on the Beat.* New York: Crowell, 1961.

Rideout, Walter B. *The Radical Novel in the United States, 1900–1945.* Cambridge, Mass.: Harvard University Press, 1956.

Simson, H. P. *Cross Currents.* New York: Harper, 1959.

Stegner, Wallace. *The Writer in America.* Tokyo: Hokuseido Press, 1953.

Stone, Wilfred H., ed. *Form and Thought in Prose.* New York: Ronald, 1954.

Tate, Allen. *Collected Essays.* Denver: Swallow, 1959.

Thorp, Willard. *American Writing in the Twentieth Century.* Cambridge, Mass.: Harvard University Press, 1960.

Trilling, Lionel. *The Opposing Self.* New York: Viking, 1955.

Warren, Robert Penn. *Selected Essays.* New York: Random House, 1958.

Wilson, Edmund. *The American Earthquake.* Garden City, N.Y.: Doubleday, 1958.